Hillel the Elder:
The Emergence
of Classical
Judaism

Hillel the Elder: The Emergence of Classical Judaism

by Nahum N. Glatzer

REVISED EDITION

A Hillel Book

SCHOCKEN BOOKS · NEW YORK

This volume is one of a series of "Hillel Little Books." Developed by the B'nai B'rith Hillel Foundations, the books in this series deal with issues of fundamental importance to Jewish college students. Written by men of variant points of view, they are intended to stimulate further study and discussion.

TO MY WIFE

ANNE

PROVERBS 31:12

CONTENTS

INTRODUCTION

A study of Hillel the Elder is essential for an understanding of the first pre-Christian century and the period preceding the destruction of the Temple in 70 C. E., an era of decisive importance in Jewish history. The study is based on talmudic and midrashic sources (some legendary) and on background information found in the Apocrypha and the Dead Sea sectarian writings.

We apply the term "classical" to the period of Hillel (who is never called "rabbi") because it was then, and not in biblical times, that a central line, a point of departure — and return — for all forms of Judaism yet to come was established. The main developments of the preceding generations — the biblical prophetic, legal, historical, early hasidic — culminate in Hillel; his work gives direction to the generations after him.

Classical Judaism, as it emerges in the Land of Israel in Hillel's time, has the vivid intensity and fascination of youth. It could still communicate with the neighboring world, could adapt freely, without losing ground, some Greek ideas, could reject freely, as it rejected "Rome." To encounter this freedom of movement in Hillel and his disciples is a refreshing experience. With the decline and fall of Antiquity (still within the talmudic era), the classical period came to an end. Later, Judaism perfected some of its tenets, stressed or overstressed others; still others it neglected or discarded. But the classical period has resisted the corrosion of time and remains a frame of reference for our understanding of all later developments.

In the classical period the factors emerged which help explain the Jewish people's passionate loyalty to Judaism — despite their global dispersion through the ages. Sociological factors (anti-Semitism, exclusion and exclusiveness, family bonds, the Jewish role in economic life, the theological interest of the medieval church in the continuing existence of vanquished Israel) may explain the physical continuity of Jewish survival. But the inner life of the Jew, his decision to live and survive as a Jew, has been nourished by the values of classical Judaism which emerged in Hillel's time.

I

THE HISTORICAL AND CULTURAL BACKGROUND

Herod the Great

It is startling to realize that Hillel was a contemporary of King Herod the Great (37–4 B. C. E.). In the consciousness of the Jew, Herod is vaguely remembered as the passionate, vengeful, cruel king of Jerusalem, while Hillel lives on as a humble sage and his words are still quoted in the form he spoke them.

Yet in the first pre-Christian century it was Herod who occupied the center of attention.[1]

Rome, which also controlled the Eastern Mediterranean, had raised Herod to the overlordship in Judea. His father was an Idumaean, his mother an Arabian; but since his tribe had been converted to Judaism, which had no racial attitude, Herod was considered a Jew. Julius Caesar made him governor of Judea (in 47 B. C. E.). When, later, he became King of the Jews and *rex socius*, friend and ally of Rome, many Jews resented the appointment. The battle of Actium (31 B. C. E.), which marked the final triumph of the Roman Empire, strengthened Herod's position. Augustus, whom Herod met in Rhodes, gladly accepted the shrewd king's assistance in the policing of the precarious border region. Herod broke the resistance of the Bedouins east of the Jordan and helped establish Arabia as a Roman province and a bridge between East and West. Augustus rewarded him with valuable Palestinian territories and cities, such as Jaffa, Gaza, Jericho. Herod himself restored ruined cities, built the harbor city of Caesarea, rebuilt Samaria, and fortified the stronghold of Masada. He rebuilt the Temple in Jerusalem and made it one of the wonders of the world. Herodian Palestine resembled Solomon's kingdom so far as external glory was concerned.

The great mistake of Herod's life was his marriage to Mariamne (Miriam), granddaughter of Hyrcanus II, the Hasmonean High Priest and ruler. The two families' incompatible points of view, their mutual intrigues, and Herod's wounded pride, drove the king to the murder of his Hasmonean wife's brother, her mother, her grandfather, and his own two sons by Mariamne. Finally, in a fit of jealousy, he executed Mariamne herself.

To a Hellenist despot human life meant little; it could readily be sacrificed if it served to advance his power. And Herod required power if he wanted to serve the cause of Augustus' Rome — to him the only cause worth serving, outside of personal pleasure and aggrandizement.

In his cultural activities, too, Herod followed the line of Roman civilization. He built theaters, baths, arenas, and hippodromes to house the games in honor of Augustus. He could not foster the emperor cult in Jerusalem or other Jewish cities. He therefore erected sanctuaries to the "divine" emperor in non-Jewish cities of his realm.

Herod took pains not to antagonize Jewish sensitivity. In rebuilding the Temple in Jerusalem, he followed the ancient laws. No images were displayed in the Temple or in any other public building in Jerusalem. Nor did the new coins carry human images. Occasionally, however, Herod's pagan trend broke through his surface compliance with Jewish teachings. He erected a large golden eagle over the great gate of the Temple. The young men who pulled the eagle down knew that the irate king would punish their act with death; they were ready to pay for their protest against paganism.

The Pharisees and the Sadducees

Since the period of the Maccabean struggle, the Jews in the land of Israel had been divided into two major groups: the Pharisaic and the Sadducean.

The Pharisees (*perushim*, meaning: separated from the unclean, dedicated to the sacred) constituted a popular party mostly of middle class urban origin. They were dedicated to cultivation of Torah and observance of the law. Torah, to the Pharisee, comprised both the written laws and the oral tradition. The "oral tradition" was an extension of the law of Moses which enabled people to find instruction and guidance for all situations in private and public life. The exact, even rigid, observance of the law was not designed to be a burden on people, but to create a feeling of an enduring connection with the divine giver of the law. The personal element in religion was preserved, the spiritual and ethical intent of the rituals stressed. Life was disciplined through instruction and training in synagogue and home. The Pharisees believed in the efficacy of repentance and in divine forgiveness. Their faith in an ultimate justice was expressed in their teachings of reward and punishment. They maintained a hope of resurrection and of a Messianic future.

The Sadducees (*Zedukim*, probably derived from the Solomonic chief priest, Zadok) comprised the priestly aristocracy and the wealthy landowners and merchants. They adjusted themselves to the political status of the semi-dependent Jewish state and followed a conservative trend in politics. The leadership of the Temple was in their hands; the High Priest headed the Sanhedrin, the Great Council in Jerusalem which interpreted the law. After the victory of the Hasmoneans, the democratic, progressive Pharisees gained in strength and began to participate in government and in the work of the Sanhedrin. But the Sadducean officials and the priests who claimed ancient authority as teachers and judges retained their power. They opposed the liberalizing innovations of the Pharisees and their preference for the laity. They rejected the oral law and grounded themselves in the text of the Torah, which they interpreted literally. This conservatism helped to secure the *status quo* and to counteract the spread of the more liberal Pharisaic tendencies.

While the Sadducees had their origin in the Temple hierarchy and derived their power from the central position of the priest of old, the Pharisees developed from the so-called Early Hasidim (*hasidim ha-rishonim*), who flourished in Judea shortly before Alexander the Great and, even more, in the post-Alexandrian period.

The Early Hasidim formed a free agricultural society, with its urban center in Jerusalem. In their small, non-capitalistic, non-mercantile, non-political communities in Judea, the Hasidim strove to realize the ideals of piety and loving devotion to God and man (*hasidut*) and justice (*tzedek*). The sabbatical year and its laws, the release of debts, were attempts to make justice rule in inter-personal relationships; the laws of the dues to the poor from the fields, olive-yards and vineyards followed the ancient prophetic principle of *hesed*, mercy, or loving-kindness; the strict laws against interest sought to eliminate unfair profit.

Early Jewish law, which decisively influenced the later, classical, formulation of Jewish law (*Halakhah*), had its origin in the life of these hasidic communities. Some of these laws are strikingly paralleled in the laws of Solon, the Athenian reformer; others reveal a knowledge of the laws in the classical Greek Polis, as they later appeared in Plato's *Laws*. This kinship demonstrates that the Early Hasidim, though profoundly rooted in the traditions of Israel, did not lead a life segregated from the world at large; they felt free to select from the culture of the independent Greek republics[2] whatever they felt was akin to them.

When the Maccabeans revolted against the tyranny of Seleucid Hellenism, some of the Hasidim, pacifist farmers, chose to join the fighters in order to defend their way of life and protect the community in which Torah was being realized.

Life in the Hasmonean state built upon the foundation of the Maccabean victory imposed on the Pharisean party some adjustments which were not in keeping with the ideals of the Early Hasidim. Participation in the government activities demanded compromise. The conservatism of the Sadducees and the strong position of the Temple priesthood could not be disregarded, especially since the ruling family of the Hasmoneans had attached itself to the Sadducees and followed a policy of assimilation to powerful Rome. The Pharisees tried to retain their ancient ideals as much as possible. The political and social conditions of the times forced them to emphasize a firm discipline. A certain rigidity developed even in the realm of teaching; the learned man was a master of the traditions which he faithfully transmitted to the students. The time was not opportune to a free, logical, systematic exposition of the *sources* of the traditions. This state of affairs represents Pharisaism before Hillel.

Some of the Pharisees, remembering the early hasidic way of life and thought, were not willing to adjust themselves to the Hasmonean state. And some of the priests, who saw their ideals compromised by the increased formalism of the Temple and the politicalization of the high Temple offices, left the Judean centers and formed their own communities; others joined already existing brotherhoods and monastic associations dedicated to the true heritage of Israel.

The Essenes and the Dead Sea Community

The ancient ideals of the Early Hasidim had found renewed expression in the brotherhoods of the Essenes, who lived on the western shore of the Dead Sea, and in the related Dead Sea sects, now called the Community of the Covenant. The Essenes are known to us from the descriptions of the philosopher Philo[3] and the historian Flavius Josephus[4] who had spent three years with an Essene as a youth and had lived the life of an Essene ascetic. Recent discoveries in the Dead Sea region inform us about the Covenanters and their writings, among them the so-called *Manual of Dis-*

cipline, a *Habakkuk Commentary*, *The War of the Sons of Light with the Sons of Darkness*. Fragments of a *Zadokite Document* which originated in the so-called Damascus Covenant are related to the Dead Sea sectarian movement and were already known.

The Essenes (some see the origin of the name in the term *hasid*) numbered about four thousand men in Hillel's time; they required several years of preparation and probation before bestowal of full membership. The new member swore that

> he will exercise piety toward God;
> observe justice towards men;
> do no harm to any one . . .;
> he will abhor the wicked and be helpful to the good;
> show fidelity to all men . . .;
> he will be a lover of truth and reprove those who tell lies;
> he will keep his hands clear from theft
> and his soul from unlawful gains . . . .[5]

As Philo put it, "they take for their standards these three: love of God, love of virtue, love of men."[6]

The Essenes lived in a communality of worldly possessions. They supported themselves by agriculture and handicraft; did not engage in commerce; and, though living in a world in which the slave was a necessary part of economy, rejected slavery "for its injustice in outraging the law of equality." Their food they ate at solemn community meals. The main group of Essenes opposed marriage; there was, however, another Essene order which permitted marriage. There are parallels between the Essene way of life and that of the religious society of the Pythagoreans, a source of some of Plato's teachings.

Because of the Essenes' neutrality in political matters, those in power in Jerusalem left them alone and treated them, in Philo's words, "as self-governing and free men and extolled that ineffable sense of fellowship, which is the clearest evidence of a perfect and happy life."

An Essene, Menahem, was on friendly terms with young Herod before the latter became king; out of regard for Menahem, Herod "continued to honor all the Essenes."

The Community of the Covenant practiced virtues similar to those of the Essenes. The members of the Community, which settled a few miles south of Jericho on the shores of the Dead Sea, shared not only in material goods, food, property, and fruits of labor, but in the exercise of good deeds as well. The *Manual of Discipline* teaches:

> They all shall live in true unity and good humility
> And loving devotion [*hesed*] and righteous purpose
> each toward his fellow in the Holy Council and as
>   members of the eternal assembly.
> They shall practice truth, unity and humility,
> Righteousness, and justice, and loving devotion
> And walking humbly in all their ways.[7]

Hesed is the basis of one's duty toward one's fellow man:

> I will repay no man with evil's due;
> Only with good will I pursue a man:

For with God is the judgment of every living thing,
And He will reward a man with his due . . . .
I will [practice] loving devotion toward the humble,
And strengthen the hands of the timid in heart
And teach understanding to the straying of spirit.

Side by side with the emphasis on ethical living, the
Essenes stressed ritual purity, purification rites, and
baptisms. The Covenanters, in addition, concentrated
on an interpretative study of the Torah; a method of
exegesis (*midrash, pesher*) helped to connect the laws
and teachings with the biblical word. This pursuit
secured a living continuity with the generations past;
it counteracted the perils which might have been a
corollary of the sects' physical separation from the
body of the people. The sectarian communities considered themselves the true Israel and looked upon the
Pharisees and Sadducees in the official centers of Judea
as compromisers with Evil who could have no future.

The trend of going into the wilderness continued
well into the early Christian period. It explains much
of the intensity of the period's religious life. Yet both
Judaism and Christianity — each in its own form —
had to find ways of constructing, or reconstructing, a
strong center while accepting the challenge of the sects.
For Judaism this meant finding the way back to
Jerusalem and reorganizing the Pharisaic party from
within. This, it appears, was the decisive and far-
reaching task of Hillel the Elder.

II

HILLEL'S BEGINNINGS
AND HIS ASCENT

Student Years

Little is known of Hillel's life. A few facts are
established; the rest must be read between the lines of
the many legends which later generations have spun
around his life.

He was born in Babylonia before the middle of the
first pre-Christian century; his father's name has not
been preserved; his mother was said to hail from the
family of King David. His education was started in
his native Babylonia; he came to Jerusalem to advance
his knowledge of Jewish tradition.[1] The time is most
probably around 40 B. C. E. when the last of the
Hasmonean princes, Antigonus Mattathiah, grandson
of King Alexander Jannaeus and Queen Salome
Alexandra, ascended the throne of Jerusalem, which,
three years later, fell into the hands of Herod.

Shemaiah and Abtalion were the leading Pharisaic
teachers in Jerusalem, and Hillel became their student.
He did manual labor — some say it was wood-cutting
— in order to support himself and his family; his wife
is praised as a person kind to the poor and steadfast in
adversity. Half of his meager daily earning was paid
as admission fee to the watchman in the house of study.
One day, the story goes, he did not find work and
the guard would not admit him without payment.

Hillel climbed up and sat upon the skylight, where he could follow the lecture. The student did not notice that snow was falling — a rare enough occurrence in Jerusalem — and was covering him. The masters finally saw him and came to his rescue.[2]

Hillel's poverty was freely chosen. It is told that his brother, Shebna, a businessman, suggested that the two become partners: Hillel was to continue his studies and Shebna was to continue earning money, while both were to share equally in the material profits from the business and the spiritual merits from learning. For the love of Torah, Hillel declined the offer and remained poor.[3]

Hillel was thoroughly trained in the traditions of Israel. For generations, Pharisaic scholars had concerned themselves with life's practical problems; they found their answers in the laws of the Torah, written and oral, transmitted by tradition. Differences of opinion were resolved by majority vote. No general principles were formulated for the interpretation of Torah.

As a student, Hillel absorbed all that his contemporaries in Jerusalem had to offer. But he must have realized that, important as this emphasis on practical issues was, it could by no means exhaust all the possible implications of Torah. The numberless regulations based on the ancient law could keep religious life under control, but they could not inspire its growth; Torah had to mean more than correct action. Even a system of ethics tends to become stale if its sources do not reveal ideal standards. A student concerned with formal exactness will turn out to be an impeccable, technically competent adviser, but not a man of the spirit. Only an academy dedicated to the narrow compass of the practical would turn away a student who cannot pay its fee and let him freeze outside if he persisted in his desire for knowledge.

Hillel must have known that much of the inquiry into Torah took place outside the Jerusalem houses of study, in the brotherhoods and monastic associations where Jews lived in accordance with the ideals of the Early Hasidim.

A New Pharisaism

Our scanty sources concerning Hillel pass in silence over a period of many years. Hillel's teachers, Shemaiah and Abtalion, have long been dead. A changed man, Hillel appears — probably around 30 B.C.E. — in the presence of the Elders of Batyra, new religious leaders in Jerusalem. They are discussing a ritual question: In case the eve of Passover fell on a Sabbath, is it permitted to sacrifice the Paschal lamb on that day, or is the prohibition of labor on the Sabbath to include the sacrifice? Nobody seems to know the tradition; Hillel, introduced as a former student of Shemaiah and Abtalion, is invited to quote the decision.

Instead of referring to a tradition, he approaches the issue by means of *midrash*, logical exposition, proving that the Passover offering overrides the Sabbath. Now, this method, having originated with the Scribes, was the method of the Covenanters. But

Hillel's attempts fail to convince the audience of the validity of his method. "He sat and expounded [*darash*] to them the whole day long but they did not accept his teaching." Finally, in despair, he exclaims: "My answer was based on a tradition from Shemaiah and Abtalion. I myself have received it from them!" That appeals to the schoolmen; they accept his ruling and appoint him to lead them from then on.[4]

Having gained a victory for the method of exposition, Hillel turned to its cultivation. Having won his audience by the reference to "tradition," he set out to train students in the reactivated method. Pharisaism had thus far conceived the oral law as a body of fixed traditions, transmitted from master to student. Hillel changed it into a movement in which Torah became the central force as the source of all law and all religious concepts. Torah was now looked upon as the perennial record of wisdom and instruction, ever ready to offer an answer to a question at hand provided the proper logical principles were applied to the text. Both historic continuity and the freedom of reasoning were safeguarded by this concept of Torah. This was a new form of Pharisaism, which we may term Neo-Pharisaism.

The exact nature of the position to which Hillel was raised is no longer known to us. The sources use the term *nasi* (prince, president) which for a long time was taken to refer to the leadership of the Great Sanhedrin, supreme council in Jerusalem for the interpretation of the law. This council, however, composed of leading priests, elders, and scribes was presided over by a high priest. After the destruction of the second Temple and the provisional leadership of Johanan ben Zakkai, we find the descendants of Hillel occupying the patriarchate which replaced the Great Sanhedrin as the official representation of Jewish Palestine up to the beginning of the fifth century. Hillel himself, it seems, was appointed head of one of the important religious commissions previously controlled by the Elders of Batyra.[5] However, Hillel's most enduring work was rooted in the school which bears his name.

Menahem the Essene and Shammai

Our sources mention a Menahem as Hillel's associate.[6] It is assumed that, later, Menahem left his office and joined the Essenes, who had influenced his thinking even before he joined them.[7] It may well be that he was an Essene before he associated with Hillel, and that he was the same Menahem the Essene whom Josephus mentioned in the story of Herod.

We don't know what brought the two men, Hillel and Menahem, together; what led Menahem, an Essene, to accept an official position in Jerusalem; and what caused him to join, or rejoin, the Essenes. But even our fragmentary information suggests that Hillel could not have been unaware of what was going on outside the official Jewish parties.

Menahem's place was taken by Shammai, a scholar who followed a more rigid line of religious and legal thought. While Hillel represented a progressive tendency, it was Shammai's office to preserve tradition. Hillel can be understood in terms of the philosophy of the Early Hasidim, Shammai in terms of the teachings of the pre-Maccabean, conservative, priesthood.[8]

At his second coming to Jerusalem Hillel was more than a preserver of tradition.[9] The determined attempt before the Elders of Batyra was indicative of a trend towards a profounder examination of the Torah as the source of Judaism.

Withdrawal and Return

Where did Hillel spend the period after leaving the college of Shemaiah and Abtalion and before his return to Jerusalem — the period shrouded in darkness in our sources? Some say he went back to Babylonia. There is nothing to substantiate such a move and a subsequent return from Babylonia to Jerusalem. A faint memory of this intermediary period seems to survive in a later reference to forty years in which Hillel (and later his disciple, Johanan ben Zakkai) "served the wise men." There is an obvious parallel between those forty years and the forty years which Moses spent in the wilderness before he was ready to lead his people into freedom.[10] We have seen that in Hillel's time many wise men lived in the wilderness where they could dedicate themselves to a life of Torah and *hasidut*, the hasidic way. Hillel's special emphasis on *hasidut* and learning after his return to Jerusalem suggest that he had gone through a period of contact with men, or groups, who lived this kind of Judaism outside the official centers.

In one of his sayings, Hillel distinguishes between periods of activity and periods in which a scholar will withdraw and but gather in knowledge. The saying reads:

When there are those who want to gather, you
    scatter (the seed of teaching);
when there are those who scatter, you gather.

That is to say:

If you see a generation to which the Torah is dear,
    you spread (its knowledge);
but if you see a generation to which the Torah is not
    dear, you gather it and keep it to yourself.[11]

Here, Hillel seems to speak out of his own experience. He himself must have withdrawn from a generation to which "the Torah was not dear" and prepared himself for a return.

An indication of the widening of the scope of Hillel's learning beyond what he had gained in his student years in Jerusalem is given in the following legendary account:

It was said of Hillel
that he had not neglected any of the words of the
    Wise but had learned them all;
he had studied all manners of speech,
even the utterance of mountains, hills and valleys,
the utterance of trees and plants,
the utterance of beasts and animals
tales of spirits, popular stories and parables,
everything he had learned.[12]

The following talmudic statement offers a clue to the nature of Hillel's activity:

> In ancient days when the Torah was forgotten from Israel,
> Ezra came up from Babylon and reestablished it.
> Then it was again forgotten
> until Hillel the Babylonian came up and reestablished it.[13]

Both Ezra the Scribe, active at the beginning of the period of the Second Commonwealth, and, four centuries later, Hillel, were preceded by periods of dissolution. In order to be effective, both, knowing the old, had to start anew. Ezra's endeavors in behalf of Torah were forgotten. Hillel aimed at reestablishing in Jerusalem a center for the *forgotten* Torah. To accomplish this, Hillel, we suggest, carefully considered the ways of the Early Hasidim and their followers in the Essene and Covenant communities. Here he found prototypes for a valid concept of Torah and its study, of law and life.

A period of communion of life with the sectarians seems probable. We venture this suggestion with all the reservation necessary as long as there is no factual evidence to support it.

One day, a group of wise men were assembled in the upper chamber of one Gurya's house in Jericho. Nothing is said about the occasion of the session, nor of what occupied the thoughts of the assembled. At one point, however, the legendary account tells that a heavenly voice announced: "There is among you one man who would deserve that the Divine Spirit rest upon him but his generation is not worthy of it." Thereupon all the eyes were fixed upon Hillel the Elder.[14]

At the basis of the legend, there seems to lie an awareness of the distance that some saw between the master and his generation. Such a feeling may have arisen when Hillel's plan to end his withdrawal and to return to Jerusalem became known to his companions. Hillel himself doubted his own powers rather than whether his people were "worthy" of his services. He may, however, have questioned whether this was the proper time "to scatter the seed of teaching" or whether he should still "keep it to himself."

"Do not separate yourself from the community"[15] was his final decision in a period of sectarianism and separatism. There was too much individualism in the sectarian groups; they considered themselves alone to be righteous; all others were "wicked." There was no bridge between the "children of light" and the "children of darkness." The sectarians led good lives, but they had forsaken Jerusalem for the better care of their own souls. Hillel thought: "If I am for myself only, what am I? And if not now, when?" He loved Jerusalem and its people, the humble and the proud, the self-satisfied and those willing to listen, the clever and the troubled. He believed in the power of the Torah to change the heart of man. "Love your fellow-man (whatever he may be) and draw him near to the Torah." He left Jericho, near which the Essenes and the Community of the Covenant were at home, and went up the road to Jerusalem.

We are now ready for a discussion of some of the central teachings to which Hillel dedicated his life: A hasidic attitude of loving concern; care for the common man and the poor; cultivation of learning and formation of a group of disciples; application of Torah to life; the search for proper ways to strengthen the community of man as opposed to the state and its power-hungry rulership; and the attempt to win proselytes for his concept of Judaism. By his activities, Hillel responded to the challenge of the sectarian movements of his time, gave a new direction to Pharisaism. In his work we witness the emergence of classical Judaism.

III

THE WAYS AND BELIEFS
OF THE HASID

We have suggested that Hillel revived some of the traditions of early Hasidism, which before and during his time had found a place of refuge in the sectarian movements. The stories of Hillel's life, the legends which formed around his activities, the sayings and teachings coming from him or attributed to him, help us to reconstruct the hasidic outlook which became an essential part of classical Judaism.[1] In our sources, the ways of Hillel are often contrasted with the ways of Shammai, Hillel's associate, who, as mentioned before, followed a more rigid approach to issues of law and religion.

> One day Hillel was returning from a journey. When he approached his neighborhood he heard cries.
> He said: I am confident that the cries do not come from my house.[2]

Here, Hillel's *hasidut* was tested. Under the circumstances, anxiety would have been a normal reaction. Not that evil cannot befall man; but the Hasid does not anticipate evil. Anxiety is conquered by trust. The recorder of the story concludes with a reference to the Psalms: "He is not afraid of evil tidings, his heart is firm, trusting in the Lord."

Every Day

> It was told of Shammai the Elder: Whenever he found a fine portion he said: This will be for the Sabbath. If later he found a finer one, he put aside the second for the Sabbath and ate the first; thus, whatever he ate, was meant for the honor of the Sabbath.
> But Hillel the Elder had a different way, for all his works were for the sake of Heaven; he used to say: "Blessed be the Lord, day by day He beareth our burden."[3]

The difference between the two men is not in their attitude to the Sabbath, revered by both, but in their attitude towards the week day. Shammai concentrated on the Sabbath, which commanded his attention during the whole week. Hillel realized that every day brought new commitments, new demands to be taken care of as if there were no other day to follow. It is man's duty to turn every single day into a blessing.

Retribution

The following is a reflection on divine justice.

Hillel saw a skull floating on the face of the water. He said to it:
Because you have drowned others, they have drowned you;
but those that drowned you will, at the last, themselves be drowned.[4]

It cannot be, Hillel thinks, that death by drowning happened by chance and had no reason. The victim must have committed a grave sin for which he suffered punishment. According to ancient belief — a motif strikingly elaborated by Franz Kafka in his story "In the Penal Colony" — the punishment can inform us about the nature of the sin. The man who was drowned must himself have drowned somebody. God employed him as his agent in executing punishment, but he could not know that he was an agent and in committing the drowning acted within his free will, for which he had to suffer the penalty of drowning. However, the first drowning and its cause remain unexplained and outside of human reasoning.

The correspondence between human and divine

action intrigued also a contemporary of Hillel, the unknown author of the *Testament of Zebulun*: "Even as a man doeth to his neighbor, even so also will the Lord do to him" which led him to this — hasidic — conclusion: "Have, therefore, compassion in your hearts."[5]

The Human Body

Not unlike the Stoics, who spoke of the kinship between man and God as a reminder to man to keep his body clean,[6] Hillel proposed to care not only for the mind but also for the body — as a religious duty.

> Once when Hillel was taking leave of his disciples, they said to him: "Master, whither are you going?"
> He replied: "To do a pious deed." They said: "What may that be?" He replied: "To take a bath." They said: "Is that a pious deed?"
> He replied: "Yes; if in the theaters and circuses the images of the king must be kept clean by the man to whom they have been entrusted, how much more is it a duty of man to care for the body, since man has been created in the divine image and likeness."[7]

In a parallel situation, Hillel answered the disciples' question:

> "I am going to do a kindness [*hesed*] to the guest in the house."
> When the disciples asked whether he had a guest every day, he answered:
> "Is not my poor soul a guest in the body? Today it is here, tomorrow it is gone."

The Essenes considered the body a prison of the soul.[8] Seneca, in part a contemporary of Hillel, spoke of the God who dwells as a guest in the human body; the Stoics often compared the soul to a guest in the body. Hillel, using a similar parable, drew the conclusion that the soul should be cared for in loving concern. As a heading for this and the preceding anecdote, the midrashic record uses Proverbs 11.17: "The man of loving-kindness [hesed] doth good to his own soul."

Beautiful Bride

Man should be truthful; "his yes should be a true yes, his no a true no";[9] a sage "whose inside is not as his outside," i. e., whose word is not sincere, "has no place in the house of study."[10] Yet does everybody wish to know the *nuda veritas*? May you deviate from sober precision to please a fellow being? There are, as usual, two schools of thought:

> What is being sung while one dances before the bride?
> The School of Shammai says: The bride is described as she is.
> The School of Hillel says: One [always] sings: "Beautiful and graceful bride!"
> Based on this the Sages say: A man's heart should always be outgoing in dealing with people.[11]

Shammai, friend of unvarnished realism, is opposed by Hillel, the Hasid.

With People

The Hasid, whom people might regard as unusual in many of his ways, will, whenever possible, live inconspicuously with people and follow the general "usage of man." Hillel said:

> Do not appear naked (among the dressed)
> neither dressed (among the naked);
> do not appear standing (among those who sit)
> neither sitting (among those who stand);
> do not appear laughing (among those who weep)
> neither weeping (among those who laugh).
> The rule is: Do not deviate from the usage of men.[12]

Patience

Another virtue of the Hasid is his forbearance. This ideal is illustrated in the well-known talmudic story:[13] Two men made a wager with each other: he who would succeed in making Hillel angry would receive four hundred *zuz*. One of the two, sure that he would win the wager, chose the most inconvenient time — Friday, the day of preparation for the Sabbath — on which to test the patience of the master. In regular intervals he appeared in Hillel's house posing not too urgent questions: "Why are the heads of the Babylonians round?" "Why are the eyes of the Palmyreans bleared?" "Why are the feet of the Africans wide?" When he received his answers he promised to come with more problems. Seeing that it was impossible to exhaust the master's patience, he asked him:

"Are you the Hillel whom they call the prince of Israel?" "Yes," answered Hillel.

The man said: "If that is you, I wish, there may not be many like you in Israel." "Why, my son?," asked Hillel. "Because I have lost four hundred *zuz* through you."

Said Hillel: "Watch out; I may cause you to lose much money but I will not easily lose my patience."

Worship

The second night of the Festival of Booths used to be celebrated on the Temple mount by a special service.[14] Hasidim and "the men of good works" mingled with the happy crowd and the music-playing Levites and contributed to the spirit of festive exuberance. They "danced before the people with burning torches in their hands singing songs and praises." Hillel's grandson (or great-grandson), Simeon ben Gamaliel, "used to juggle with eight lighted torches, throwing them and catching them without one of them touching the other."

This is the background for an enigmatic saying of Hillel in which he lets God speak:

If I am here, everyone is here;
if I am not here, who is here?

IV

THE COMMON MAN
AND THE POOR

The Rescue of the Common Man

From earliest times, Judaism has been aware of the polarity of good and evil, the righteous and the wicked, the sinners and the pure in heart. The sinners were usually identified with the rich, and the poor with the righteous and the humble. The rich enjoyed the blessings of this earth and transgressed the law when it suited their purpose; the poor trusted in their eventual triumph and in the doom of the evildoers. In the period when the Hasmoneans favored the aristocratic Sadducees, especially during the reign of Alexander Jannaeus, the tension between the "sinners" and the "righteous" grew immensely. The difference between them was both theological and socio-political. Behind the "righteous" hid the Pharisean party, behind the "wicked" the Sadducees. The rise to power of the latter seemed indicative of the political future of the country.

The Community of the Covenant and those who felt a kinship to it greatly stressed this sharp division in Israel and the world. They felt that it reflected a dualism in the universe at large. Good and Evil are absolute powers in the world. As against the realm dominated by Evil and Darkness in which the sinners live, there are the sons of the Covenant ("the Elect of

Grace"), led by the Teacher of Righteousness ("the Elect one of God").

The Book of Enoch, written probably by an author close to the sectarian thinking, forcefully expresses the hatred of the righteous and the good against the wicked, the sinners and "man-pleasers."

"Woe to you, ye rich, for ye have trusted in your riches."

"Woe to you, sinners, for ye persecute the righteous."

"Be hopeful, ye righteous; for suddenly shall the sinners perish before you."

"Blessed are all they who accept the words of wisdom . . . for they shall be saved; be hopeful ye that have died in righteousness," for whom "all goodness and joy and glory are prepared."[1]

That was the state of the problem of the just and the wicked as Hillel and his school found it. The harshness of *The Book of Enoch* mirrors the psychology of a radical sectarian group which knows only black and white, only friend or foe, righteous or wicked. But life transcends such rigid classifications. A new concept of man was needed. Especially to Hillel this contrast of black and white was incompatible with his hasidic concepts of neighborly love and mercy and with his attempts to win the common man. Hillel (and Shammai) accepted the traditional distinction between the "wholly righteous" (who are destined to eternal life) and the "thoroughly wicked" (who are doomed to ignominy). But they knew that most people were neither wholly bad nor wholly good;

what was to be their fate? The School of Shammai, disciplinarians as ever, insisted that those who did wrong would taste the purifying fire of punishment, would struggle and rise again; they were to be "refined as silver, tried as gold"; "for the Lord . . . bringeth down to the grave and bringeth up."

But this did not satisfy Hillel. Mercy!, he cried. God is the Lord of abounding mercy. For the "average man," God in his grace "inclines the scales of judgment towards grace." There is no doom, no fire of punishment for him, only divine love and forgiveness. In behalf of these people, adds the School of Hillel, David composed Psalm 116 in which it says: "Gracious is the Lord, and righteous; yea, our God is compassionate. The Lord preserveth the simple. I was brought low, and He saved me. Thou hast delivered my soul from death, mine eyes from tears, and my feet from stumbling. I shall walk before the Lord in the lands of the living."[2]

The Poor and the Humble

There is an obvious connection between the common man and the poor and humble. Hillel's early years spent in poverty determined his social attitude throughout his life; he remained devoted to the cause of the poor. His personal experience made him sensitive to the teachings of Israel which considered the poor and the humble especially beloved by God. Both appear strangely interrelated in the biblical Psalms. In the

post-Maccabean period when the group of the pros-
perous grew influential and joined forces with the
Court, the poor and the humble became, even more
than before, a special concern of religious thinking.

The Sects

Philo, in his description of the Essenes, implies a
connection between poverty and the avoidance of
injustice: "Among all men, they alone are without
money and without possessions, but are nevertheless
the richest of all, because to have few wants and to live
frugally they regard as riches. Among them is no
maker of any weapons of war . . . nor do they follow
any occupation that leads to injustice and covetous-
ness."[3] They manifested "special zeal in offering
sympathy and succor to those in distress."[4]

The Community of the Covenant preached contempt
for wealth; love of riches characterized the wicked
"men of the Pit."[5] The members of the sect call
themselves "the community of the poor."[6] The early
Judeo-Christians who followed the tradition of the
Jerusalemite Christian community called themselves
ebionim, Ebionites, the poor ones.

In the same way, *The Psalms of Solomon*, written
close to the period of Hillel's activity, speak of the
pious and the poor in parallel lines:

> And the pious shall give thanks in the assembly of
> the people;
> And on the poor shall God have mercy in the
> gladness of Israel.[7]

Hillel accepted this tradition and the emphasis put on it by the sectarian groups. He made the poor and the broken a loving concern of his private life and represented the cause of the poor in his academy as against the advocates of the older, conservative, Pharisaism and its spokesman, Shammai.

Among the stories that illustrate Hillel's regard for the poor, is the one of Hillel and his wife preparing a meal in honor of a guest and then giving it to a poor man who happened to appear at the door.[8]

The mention of Hillel's wife as participating with him in the charitable act is not a coincidence. The wife plays an important role, as illustrated in the story of another Hasid, Abba Hilkiah, and his wife, who jointly prayed for rain. "They went up to the roof; he stood in one corner and she in another; at first the clouds appeared over the corner where his wife stood." Later he explained: "Because a wife stays at home and gives bread to the poor which they can at once use while I give them money which they cannot at once enjoy."[9]

Hillel believed that loving-kindness must take into account the particular situation in which the poor man finds himself.

> There was a man of a wealthy family who had become poor.
> Hillel provided him with a horse to ride upon and with a servant to run before him.
> One day he could not find a servant, so he himself ran before him for three miles.[10]

A Midrash expounding the laws of charity refers to this and a similar episode, and adds:

> "Be careful that you withhold not pity, for he who withholds pity from his fellow man is likened by Scripture to a worshipper of idols, and he throws off the yoke of heaven."[11]

Humility

Hillel said:

My humiliation is my exaltation;
My exaltation is my humiliation.[12]

This means: He who humbles himself will be exalted; he who exalts himself will be humbled and will fall. If provoked the Hasid will remain silent. His God is silent, too. "He who hears himself cursed and remains silent, although he has the means to protest, becomes a partner of God: He hears the pagan nations blaspheme him and he keeps silent.[13] A Midrash defines men who love God as

those who are humiliated but humiliate not,
those who hear themselves shamed but do not answer,
who act out of love
and rejoice in their sufferings.[14]

Everyman

A man of few words, Hillel did not engage in preaching social justice. But we see him meeting Everyman, and especially the needy, in a spirit of complete equality. The poor, as Hermann Cohen once said, is the arch-type of Everyman; man is revealed in the poor man. And we see Hillel making room for the poor and the humble in the social laws and in religious custom. The sects in the desert were no longer the sole brothers of the poor. Through Hillel's activity, concern for the poor became a central motif of classical Judaism.

V

LEARNING

Hillel introduced a new note into the house of study. We say introduced, not invented. We do find traces of this new type of learning in Judea before Hillel; we find a strong emphasis on, and a cultivation of, this learning in the sectarian movements of the time. Through Hillel, it seems, this emphasis and culture were transplanted from the isolation of the sectarian associations into the schools of Jerusalem.

We will first turn our attention to the place of study in the sectarian movements, then come back to Hillel.

Learning in the Sectarian Movements

In the Essene community we encounter special meetings for the study of sacred writings. Philo tells us that the Essenes at all times "study industriously the ethical part (of philosophy)," particularly on the

Sabbath. The group follows the discourse of the master. Study enables a husband "to transmit knowledge of the laws" to his wife, the father to his children, the master to his servant.[1]

The *Manual of Discipline* tells us that the men of the Community of the Covenant gave a third of all the nights of the year to the study of the Torah. In any given group of ten men there should always be one "who expounds the Law day and night, continually.[2]

The *Manual* quotes Isaiah 40.3, "Clear ye in the wilderness the way of the Lord." This "way" is defined as "the study of the law" [*midrash ha-torah*].[3] The community, led by an "interpreter (or searcher) of the Torah" [*doresh ha-torah*],[4] studied the teachings in common, in a process in which the mind and the heart, the intellectual, spiritual and emotional faculties took part. Study here was a sacred action; a connection was perceived between knowledge and piety. Through study, the Torah revealed something of the "way of the Lord" in the affairs of the world and of man. Study though pursued in community is a highly individual affair; it is one of man's links with the divine and thus a mystery. Our *Manual* speaks of the "true knowledge" which will be gained by those who have chosen the Way.[5]

To the Community of the Covenant this pursuit of knowledge and piety cannot take place in the midst of the people who have made peace with the corrupt world around them. "This is the time of clearing the way to go to the wilderness," the *Manual* states.[6]

Hillel: The Ignorant Cannot be a Hasid

The culture of the Dead Sea sects was, we assume, known to Hillel. But he did not think that this culture should flourish only in the wilderness. True, few were left in Jerusalem to do the work. But "in a place where a man is needed and there is none, try to be a man." Here Hillel voiced his wish to reestablish the deserted center of learning in Judea. "The ignorant cannot be a Hasid"; the sectarians knew this and acted accordingly in their retreats. Hillel wanted to battle ignorance — in Jerusalem.

Even before his time it had been taught: "Raise up many disciples," "Let your house be a meeting house for the wise"; the masters' responsibilities towards their disciples had been recognized.[7] But studies mainly meant studies of the established traditions. Now, however, a new form of learning was needed and a new kind of relationship between master and disciple. Only in the School of Hillel do we find this true community of disciples and the communion of learning.

Some of Hillel's sayings, though touching also on other motifs, mainly emphasize the theme of study.

First let us consider the entire saying, parts of which we have quoted before:

> The uneducated knows not fear of sin;
> the ignorant cannot be a Hasid.
> The timid is not apt to learn,
> the impatient is not fit to teach.

He whose whole time is absorbed in business will
not attain wisdom.

In a place where (a man is needed and) there are no
men, try to be a man.[8]

There is an intimate relationship between learning,
personal ethics, and the attitude toward one's fellow-
man:

Do not separate yourself from the community.

Trust not yourself until the day of your death.

Judge not your fellow-man before you have come
into his situation.

Say not a thing that cannot be understood at once in
the assumption that sometime in the future it will
be understood.

Say not: "When I shall have leisure I shall study";
perhaps you will not have leisure.

The warning against absorption in business is followed by a warning against yielding to temptations of
material achievement at the expense of study:

Hillel used to say:

The more flesh, the more worms;
the more possessions, the more worry;
the more women, the more witchcraft;
the more maid-servants, the more immorality;
the more men-servants, the more thieving.

But:

The more Torah, the more life;
the more study and contemplation, the more wisdom;
the more counsel, the more discernment;
the more charity, the more peace.

And:

A good name, once acquired, is your own possession;
he who has knowledge of the Torah has life in the
  world to come.

Learning requires selflessness and constant care:

A name made famous is a name lost.
Knowledge that does not grow will shrink.
He who refuses to teach faces death.
He who uses the crown of learning for material gain
  vanishes.

In explaining the first line of this saying, the sages
remark: "If a man makes himself great, he is not
really great, unless one greater than he has made
him great." [9]

The man of learning will attempt to gain disciples
from among the simple and the humble:

How did Hillel bring his fellow-man near to the
  Torah?
One day Hillel stood in the gate of Jerusalem and
  met people going out to work.
He asked: "How much will you earn to-day?"
One said, A denarius; the other said, Two denarii.
He asked them: "What will you do with the
  money?"
They gave answer: "We will pay for the necessities
  of life."
Then he said to them:
"Why don't you rather come with me and gain
  knowledge of the Torah,
that you may gain life in this world
and life in the world-to-come?"

Thus Hillel was wont to do all his days and has
brought many under the wings of Heaven.[10]

Hillel's method of starting a conversation reminds
us of the Stoics and the Cynics and, of course, of
Socrates. He refers to the occupation of the one
spoken to; it is this person's terminology and mode of
thinking which Hillel uses in order to let him discover
for himself what the right thing is.

Learning is worship, indeed. And as worship is not
confined to special times and occasions but pervades
the whole of man's conscious life, so learning has to
be continual. The prophet Malachi speaks of the
distinction "between him that serveth God and him
that serveth Him not." "He that serveth Him not,"
Hillel explained, is the one who had studied but had
ceased to do so; only he who studies without cessation
is the one "that serveth God."[11]

Nomos in Hellenism

Our analysis of learning would not be complete
without an attempt to describe the scope of Torah,
or Law.

The Septuagint, the Greek translation of the Hebrew
Bible, renders the word Torah usually by the Greek
word *nomos*, which means law. To later users "Law"
suggested a collection of statutes, commandments and
injunctions. The importance of laws for the welfare
of a society was readily recognized, but beyond that
the term yielded no deeper significance.

Yet when the Greek-speaking world used the word *nomos*, the term meant a great deal. To the Stoics, Law suggested primarily a cosmic, universal law. The Hellenist thinker found the true law only in the cosmos.[12] The law which governed the universe was valid also for the community of men and for the gods. The *nomos*, being the highest reason (*logos*), ruled both in nature and in man's moral action. This universal law was divine. What law, in the narrow sense, meant for the state, God was to the world; some identified God with the universal order.

Man follows his inborn reason in making his commitment for *nomos* and for a life according to *nomos*. It is man's nature and his destiny to fulfil the law; thus, man reaches true freedom. In obeying the law, man lives according to nature, which is a Stoic ideal; he becomes happy and beloved of God; in following the law, man follows God.

In the Hellenist world the term *nomos* in its broad application roughly carried the range of meaning that the term Torah conveyed to the Jew. In translating *nomos* as law we are philologically correct, but in applying the term law to Torah, we are considerably narrowing down its meaning.

Torah in Judaism

Reminiscent of the position of *nomos* in the Stoa, the Jew sees in the Torah a cosmic, universal force. Tradition has it that the creation of the Torah preceded the creation of the world;[13] before creating the world,

God looked into the Torah. The meaning which it established was valid not only for man but also for nature and for the universe. God Himself is described as studying the Torah. In principle, the validity of the Torah is not limited to Israel. It was not given in the Land of Israel but on Sinai, in the wilderness between Egypt and the Land of Israel, thus "in public, for all to see, in the open, and everyone who wishes to receive it, let him come and receive it." To emphasize the universal character of the Torah, the revelation took place in the seventy languages of mankind, but the nations of the world were not ready to accept it. In accepting the Torah, Israel has made peace between God and His world. The Torah charges man with many responsibilities; in fulfilling them he becomes free.

These views upheld by the Palestinian masters are paralleled by Philo of Alexandria. Philo sees a basic harmony between Torah and reason, cosmos and nature, all rooted in the oneness of God. To the perfect man the Torah is the expression of divine reason and wisdom which a man will choose to follow — in freedom.[14]

Halakhah

In a more definite sense Torah, law, represents to classical Judaism the expression of God's will. Once declared on Sinai, this will is now recorded in the Torah in human language. Since God is not primarily law-giver but father, creator, lover of His creatures and of His people, the pronouncement of His will inspires ready acceptance. By living according to Halakhah — the classical Jewish term for the law — the Jew overcomes the chaos which threatens human life; he emerges victorious over anarchy and establishes order in himself. There is no sphere which can be considered irrelevant. Everything in life, big and small, is given form and significance by Halakhah.

The examination of the written law — the Torah — is pursued along logical, rational lines. Hillel is known to have promulgated the so-called "seven rules" or norms of interpretation which were expanded by later sages.

As an example we may mention the rule of "generalization of a special law" (*binyan av*, literally, the formation of a leading regulation). The law states: "No man shall take the mill or the upper millstone to pledge; for he taketh a man's life to pledge."[15] The law clearly states that only these objects were not to be used as security for debts. However, confiscation of other objects could equally jeopardize a man's life. Therefore, Hillel's rule provides that the special law may be generalized. It implies "everything which is used for the preparation of food." Unless a biblical law appears directed to a particular case, it is examined as to its general validity.

This system of exposition made it possible to apply the law liberally to new conditions of time and society. Thus, everything could be found in the Torah; a tradition in law or custom did not have to rest on a school regulation or on legal enactment but could be traced back to its origin in the Torah. In this point Hillel's activity was decisive.[16]

The Aim of Learning

The term "learning," or study of the Torah, is so frequently used that our ears are dulled to its meaning. We must attempt to redefine it. True, there had been instruction in Israel since biblical days and there were occasions when the Torah was read and explained in public. But it was only in the last generations before Hillel that the learning of the Torah became a principal force in Judaism: First, in the sectarian movements and in the Diaspora, then, through Hillel, in Jerusalem and in classical Judaism.

Learning is more than the sum of the portions studied. The very process of immersion into the biblical word is more than a quest for information. Learning ultimately aims not at "practical," usable knowledge. The study of the Torah is only outwardly the study of a book; actually it is the study of the divine thought. There is no "new" revelation; there are no longer prophets in Israel who would utter a new divine word; but through dedicated learning, the learner will understand anew the word spoken on Sinai. This understanding is the aim of learning.

VI

THE TWO RIVAL
SCHOOLS

Hillel and Shammai

In their interpretation of the law, Hillel and his
followers were known to be forbearing, Shammai and
his followers to be uncompromising. The differences
between the two schools were based not so much on
personal leanings as on different social and economic
factors.[1] Hillel and the Hillelites identified themselves
with the poor, or, at any rate, the less privileged groups
of the population, the Plebeians, while Shammai and
his school represented the interests of the well-to-do,
the Patricians. Hillel was the spokesman of the common people and advocated progressive trends, Shammai
advanced the concerns of the conservatives, the tradi-
tionalists, the aristocratic families — and the priestly
group.

As against the Shammai trend which, continuing an
older Pharisaic tradition, wanted to restrict admission
to the Schools to students who were not only wise and
modest but also of good family and rich, Hillel and his
followers, initiators of a Neo-Pharisaism, maintained
that "one ought to teach every man"[2] — rich and
poor.

The following discussions of religious usage — they may seem trifles to some — will show us Hillel's resolve to accommodate the poor.

At the home service on the eve of the Sabbath or of a festival certain benedictions are recited. The School of Shammai taught that first the benediction be recited over the sanctity of the day and then over the wine; the School of Hillel maintained that the benediction should first be recited over the wine and then over the day.[3] The suggested sequences were not a matter of formal legalism; they were based on economic differences in the population. The well-to-do were used to having wine on the table even on weekdays. Wine was no distinctive feature on a festive day and thus the "benediction over the day" had to come first to declare the special character of the season. The poor, on the other hand, to whom wine was a symbol of festivity, would fitly commence the Sabbath home service by saying the blessing over the wine and follow this by an affirmation of the sanctity of the day.

Another example: According to the School of Shammai, the so-called New Year for fruit-trees is observed on the first day of the Hebrew month of Shevat; according to the School of Hillel, on the fifteenth.[4] The reason for the difference in date is economic: The rich have better fields and gardens and their fruits mature earlier than the produce of the gardens of the poor. Shammai and his school represented the rich, Hillel and his school the poor.

Hillel's accent on human dignity can be seen in his opinion on problems of family law.

According to the law of the Torah, a father could give his daughter in betrothal while she was still in her girlhood, i. e., up to twelve and a half years of age.[5] If married off by some other relative (her father being dead) the daughter, before reaching majority, could exercise her "right of refusal" and be set free. Shammai ruled that a girl could exercise this right only as long as she was betrothed but not yet married. Hillel, however, allowed refusal both to the betrothed and the married. As against the opinion that the refusal must be exercised before the court and in the presence of the husband, Hillel stated that neither a court session nor the husband's presence was required. Hillel even permitted a girl to exercise her right of refusal before she came of age. Without changing the biblical law, Hillel removed any vestige of coercion which could have disturbed married life.

Biblical law permits a man to divorce his wife "if he hath found some unseemly thing in her" and provides for a bill of divorcement. Post-biblical legislation saw the necessity to restrict the husband's right to divorce his wife. The School of Shammai allowed a divorce only on grounds of unchastity. Those who believed that marriages were made in heaven were not too eager to dissolve them on less impressive grounds. Hillel felt that a rigid divorce law would be detrimental to a peaceful family life and opposed any restriction; his view made a voluntary dissolution of marriage possible.

In the context of marriage laws the School of Shammai taught that if a bill of divorce had been written out and the couple continued to live together, the bill may still be used. Or, if a man divorced his wife and she then lodged with him in an inn, she does not need another bill of divorce from him. Hillel forbade this and, in both cases, required another bill of divorce. Here Hillel appears to be more strict than Shammai, but in truth he only shows greater regard for the human situation. Lodging together might have reconciled the couple, for the time being at least, and this renders the bill of divorce, written under different circumstances, obsolete. Here more and not less formality may be helpful to the wavering couple.

Controversial Books

The book *Ecclesiastes* (Kohelet), written not without some awareness of Hellenist thought, expresses skepticism against certain tenets of traditional religion. The unknown author examines human existence and the functioning of society and cannot detect a purpose. Events seem predetermined; the search for truth is futile. The present is vain, the future will be but a dull rehash of the past. The good and the wicked alike are ruled by chance; there is no reward, and no justice; all is vanity.

The Schools of Hillel and Shammai discussed the question whether or not *Ecclesiastes* should be considered a part of the Bible. At that time the canon of Scriptures was not yet closed and the eligibility of certain books was still being discussed. The Shammai school, pointing to many contradictions in the book, opposed its inclusion; the Hillelites advocated its inclusion; in spite of its contradictions, the book is Torah. Midrashic exegesis could be applied to tone down the passages of blunt pessimism. In doing so, the reader might miss the literal meaning of the text, but the book as such would be carefully preserved as a part of Scriptures and would be saved from oblivion.[6]

The book of the prophet Ezekiel was also in danger of exclusion. The Shammaitic conservatives felt that in some laws regulating priestly activity the book contradicted the precepts of the Pentateuch. But the liberal Hillelite tradition attracted the very leader of the Shammaitic school who, we are told, withdrew into the solitude of an upper chamber until he resolved the contradictions; thus he could help preserve the book of the prophet who taught the individual responsibility of man.[7]

On Creation and Man's Existence

The debates between the schools included also theological and ethical questions. Quite often the view taken on a theological issue reveals a person's attitude to life and to the world around him. Speaking of Creation — one of the great themes in the first pre-Christian century and later — the School of Shammai gave precedence to "heaven" and all it implies, the School of Hillel to "earth." The discussion between the various groups continued, until later sages determined to view both heaven and earth as equally great acts of One creation.[8]

"Is it good that man has been created or would it be better if he had not been created?" This question, according to the Talmud, occupied the two rival schools for two and a half years. The School of Hillel took the optimistic, life-affirming side, the School of Shammai the opposing view. Finally, both schools agreed that it was futile to discuss whether non-existence "would have been" better. Theoretically, Hillel may grant this much to Shammai. But man's existence is a fact; assuming this, all he can do is to make the best of his life and carry his responsibility as ably as possible.

Hillel's Victory

Although the two schools were in disagreement on a number of questions, even on questions of marriage law and family status, the two groups of scholars did not abstain from marrying women of the other school. "This is to teach you that they practiced love and friendship toward one another, thus fulfilling what is said: 'Love ye truth and peace.' "[9]

While originally the followers of the respective schools adhered to the opinions and rulings laid down by their leaders, it was decided later on to unify the law; in most cases preference was accorded to the teachings of Hillel and his school. To quote the Talmud:

The words of both schools are the words of the
  living God,
but the law follows the rulings of the School of
  Hillel
because the Hillelites were gentle and modest,
and studied both their own opinions and the opinions
  of the other school,
and humbly mentioned the words of the other school
  before theirs.
The preference accorded to the School of Hillel
  teaches you
that he who humbles himself the Lord raises up,
and he who exalts himself the Lord humbles;
greatness flees him who seeks greatness;
greatness may follow him who flees from greatness;
he who (impatiently) tries to force time, is thrown
  back by time;
he who (patiently) yields to time, finds time standing
  by him.[10]

The debates between Hillel and Shammai serve as
an example of "a controversy that is in the name of
Heaven." Even if they don't prevail, the opinions of
Shammai and Hillel have been recorded, as the Mishnah
says, "to teach the generations to come that none should
persist in his opinion, for these 'fathers of the world'
did not persist in their opinions."

Thus it was Hillel's refusal to exercise power
(beyond the power inherent in an honest and truthful
utterance) that led to the recognition of his authority
in the Jewish community. It was recognized that
Shammai, too, represented "the word of God" — but
it was a very personal matter that militated against
him and his school: his lack of humility.

There is a tragic postscript to this ideal attempt. In the course of time the gentlemanly discussions between the schools deteriorated. Debates were no longer aimed solely at finding a solution to a problem or at arriving at an understanding of a text. Instead, the students tended to display their skill in the techniques of scholarship. Irrelevant "disputes multiplied in Israel and the one Torah became as two Torahs."

VII

COMMUNITY VS. STATE

The reader will do well to keep in mind that all we have discussed this far took place in the city of Herod and the Herodians. The warm humanity and passion for mercy we have described, stand in sharp contrast to the pomp, power and violence of the contemporary rulers of Jerusalem. Hillel could not accept Herod's state. Nor would he engage in a futile struggle against it. He used his strength and wit for constructive work in behalf of that other form of association of men which had been realized by the Early Hasidim: the community. As against the state, Hillel, and after the destruction of the Temple, his disciple Johanan ben Zakkai, built the *community* on the free and peaceful collaboration of its members.

The community in turn created a dynasty of its own in Hillel's family. Hillel was considered the prince of

the community and the people looked upon him as
their secret counter-king, the legitimate ruler opposed
to Herod the usurper.[1]

This shift in emphasis from the rule of kings to the
guidance by a teacher, from state to community,
manifested itself in new communal ideals and practices.
A few illustrations follow.

Peace

Hillel said:

Be of the disciples of Aaron (the priest),
loving peace, pursuing peace.
Be one who loves his fellow-creatures
and draws them near to the Torah.[2]

For a century, up to Herod, the most prominent
representatives of the family of Aaron the priest had
been the Hasmonean rulers. Their activities came to
be associated with wars of defense, wars of conquest,
intrigue, ruthless pursuit. Against this distorted picture
of Aaron, Hillel tried to reconstruct the old, prophetic,
image of the priest who was a man of peace and whose
example may be emulated by all. Hillel's sentence
implies a criticism of politics as understood by the
official spokesmen of his time; it does not imply
quietism. "Loving peace" has a passive ring in it;
"pursuing peace" calls for activity. Hillel's disciple,
Johanan ben Zakkai, explained the master's words.
They mean: establish peace between a man and his
neighbor, between husband and wife, between family

and family, between city and city, between nation and nation, between government and government.[3] Peace among nations will be but an extension of the peace between a man and his neighbor. To Hillel, peace both in the home and in the world is based on one factor; love of fellow-man: "The more charity, the more peace."

Hillel's position was presaged by the a-political stand of another Hasid, Onias. During the battles between the two Hasmonean brothers, Hyrcanus II and Aristobulus II, Onias was asked by Hyrcanus' followers to pray for the fall of the forces of Aristobulus. At first Onias refused to act but when the crowd tried to force him he stood up and prayed:

> O God, the king of the whole world!
> Since those who stand now with me are Thy people
> and those that are besieged are also Thy priests,
> I pray
> that Thou mayest not listen to the prayers of those
>   against these,
> nor bring to effect what these pray against those.

Those near him were greatly dismayed by his impartiality and stoned him to death in order to prevent a further demonstration of such an attitude.[4]

Obviously, a man who was concerned with justice and was not willing to compromise, could not support either political party. On the other hand, those who expected a solution from either party could not show tolerance for a man who rejected both because he accepted both as children of God.

Unlike the Dead Sea sects who forsook the community of Israel at large, we find Hillel actively engaged in improving the conditions of the community and in initiating special legislative measures [*takkanot*] in its behalf. One such enactment is known as *prosbul* (from the Greek *prosbolē*, or *prosboulē*, which means, before the council) and refers to a social reform for the protection of both borrowers and creditors.

The biblical law of the Sabbatical year[5] required that all loans be remitted in that year. The intention of this law was to protect the small farmer; it was beneficent in a simple agricultural society. It tried to prevent the accumulation of property in the hands of a few successful men and the increase of economically dependent landholders. However, in the more advanced economy of post-biblical times, credit was not confined to the poor; commerce was dependent on the flow of credit. Creditors were reluctant to extend loans when the Sabbatical year was approaching, for fear of not getting them back in time and thus losing them entirely. The law which appeals to the heart ("thou shalt not harden thy heart, nor shut thy hand from thy needy brother . . . thou shalt surely lend him sufficient for his need") and which was supposed to prevent destitution, had achieved the opposite. The situation became especially acute when at the beginning of Herod's rule the land suffered a series of poor harvests and the need for loans was keenly felt.

Hillel, adopting a Hellenistic institution, introduced

the *prosbul*, which consisted in a handing over of the bonds to the court and in a declaration in court by which the creditor retained the right to collect his debts even after the Sabbatical year. Thus the creditor was protected against cancellation and the poor borrower did not have to fear the resistance of the lender. The ancient sources say that this reform (which implied a modification of a specific biblical law) was introduced "for the better order of society."

Another legal enactment by Hillel referred to the sale of houses in a walled city. According to the biblical law, real estate in general, if sold, returned to the original owner in the fiftieth year, the "year of the jubilee." This regulation did not apply to houses in a walled city. Such houses, however, could be bought back ("redeemed") by the original owner in the course of one year. In Hillel's time buyers used to circumvent this law by absenting themselves around the time when the original owner could be expected to make his bid; thus the new landlord could enjoy his property forever and the original owner missed his chance to regain the property to which he was attached. Hillel restored this privilege by a legal measure which allowed the original owner to deposit the amount due in the court of law, and thus retain the right to renewed ownership.

Enactments such as this and the *prosbul* show Hillel's concern with the social problems of his day. His reforms, utilizing public, legal institutions for the benefit of the individual member of society, were not envisaged as final solutions of social problems —

which ultimately were human problems. But they offered a basis for an improvement of life in a community where little help was to be expected from the state. An escape into the desert was a step in the wrong direction. "Do not separate yourself from the community." One cannot redeem the community by withdrawing from it.

The Jar of Oil

The attitude of the schools to the Maccabean revolt and the Hasmonean kingdom is expressed in the symbolism connected with the festival of Hanukkah.

The tradition to kindle one light on the first night of Hanukkah, two on the second, and so on up to eight, goes back to the School of Hillel. The School of Shammai, following a different reasoning, kindled eight lights on the first night and reduced them as the nights went by.[6]

The usage of the School of Hillel is followed until this day. However, both Hillel and Shammai perpetuated the emphasis on the miracle of the small jar of oil which was found in the newly-dedicated Sanctuary and which lasted eight days until the new oil was ready for use. This event and what it symbolized took the center of the Maccabean story, and not the victory of the Hasmonean fighters. Hillel's descendant, the Patriarch Judah, omitted from his *Mishnah* any reference to the political side of the Hanukkah story. The Maccabean heroes gave rise to the Hasmonean kings, who usurped the throne of David, and finally gave way to the Hellenist kingdom of Herod. Herod's contemporaries, Hillel and Shammai, heirs of the traditions of Hasidism and of ancient priesthood, used the symbol of the humble jar of oil as the expression of their non-political stand, their choice of a non-violent resistance to the sword and their determination to go the way of gentleness.

Messianism

Hillel's teachings are silent about the Messianic idea which, proclaimed by the prophets, took on acute and urgent forms in the writings of apocalyptic visionaries like Daniel, who wrote during the Maccabean rebellion. Impatient believers wanted to force the hand of Providence and to hasten the expected end. Hillel, the patient teacher, assumed an attitude of restrained waiting when he thought of the future. The field of action was to him not the future — the great theme of Messianism — but the present and its transfiguration according to the word of God: this life had to be lived to the full.

But the yearning for Messianic redemption grew stronger in these last decades before, and the first decades of, the common era, in the Near East and in the Roman world at large. The fourth eclogue of Virgil, influenced by Oriental ideas, speaks of the advent of a new era and of the birth of a miraculous redeemer of suffering humanity. The Covenanters have, for some time, been living in concrete anticipation of the Kingdom of God. Soon after Hillel, Judea witnessed the rise of Jesus' Messianic community.

The people of Judea were not united in attitude. Dissension must have risen to immense proportions during Hillel's last years and after his death. The controversies revolved around the Messianic visions of the biblical prophets and the meaning of their words.

Jonathan ben Uzziel, Hillel's disciple whose method of studying Scripture was believed to dispel all doubts and ambiguities,[7] is said to have undertaken an Aramaic translation (*Targum*) of the prophetic books. He approached the task of an interpretative translation of the much-debated books as an answer to the challenge of the time. His work is not preserved. Tradition, however, makes him heir to the teachings of the last prophets who in the initial period of the Second Commonwealth represented a Messianic trend. There was strong criticism of Jonathan's work and a voice (in which we recognize the tone of Hillel) demanded: "Who is this that has revealed the Lord's secrets to man?" Whereupon Jonathan rose to his defense: "It is I who have revealed God's secrets to man. I have not done this for my own honor but for the honor of God, that dissension may not increase in Israel!" He went on with his work, which was to lead him into the vision of the *Book of Daniel* with its allusions to the Messianic end of days. Again the voice issued and said: No more![8]

In these veiled references we hear the echo of the distrust of speculations which went hand-in-hand with the fervent hopes for the Messianic change of events.

Underlying this distrust was the knowledge of the explosive nature of Messianism. Hillel's way was the study of the Torah; the life of Halakhah (discipline) and *hasidut* led towards the Kingdom of God on earth growing slowly through the ages. "Blessed be the Lord, day by day."

Herodianism and Zealotism (a Note on Toynbee)

In his *A Study of History*, Arnold Toynbee paints with bold strokes "the historic collision between Hellenism and Jewry" and "the pressure exerted by Hellenism . . . upon Jewry on every plane of social activity . . . ."[9] The only choice to meet this challenge was, according to Toynbee, the one between Herodianism and Zealotism. Herod the Great had offered to the Jews "a mundane solution of their Hellenic problem:" to realize "this alien social force's irresistibly superior power," to assimilate, then to lead "a more or less comfortable life in the Hellenizing World that was their inescapable new social environment." The Herodians saw in Hellenism "a hard fact . . . from which there was no possibility of escape."

To the other attitude towards Hellenism, Toynbee applies the term Zealotic. The Zealots in trying "to fend off the formidable aggressor" retreated "into the spiritual fastness of their own Jewish heritage . . . maintained an unbroken and unbending front" hoping to be "given grace to draw from the jealously guarded source of their own spiritual life a supernatural strength that would enable them to repel the alien aggressors."

The Herodians, Toynbee says, would consider "the Zealots' attitude of uncompromising non-recognition of the presence and power of this triumphant alien force . . . an attitude of moral cowardice entailing an impolicy of impossibilism that courted certain defeat." The Herodians, advocates of "voluntary Hellenization of Jewish life," saw in the way of the Zealots "a stupidly purposeless sacrifice."

Toynbee uses the term Zealotism both for "the way of Violence," i. e., the Jewish military resistance to the Hellenist conqueror (in the years 66–70; 115–117; 132–135 C. E.) and for "the way of Gentleness" as represented by Johanan ben Zakkai. At the fall of the Temple this sage had placed *hesed*, the great principle of the Early Hasidim and of Hillel, at the center of the surviving Jewish community. Both Hillel and Johanan ben Zakkai had radically renounced the sword and the exercise of power as incompatible with *hesed*. Toynbee knows this; he speaks of Johanan ben Zakkai as "the founder of a new Jewry which has survived" and adds: "The secret of this latter-day Jewry's extraordinary survival power lies in its persistent cultivation of the ethos which Johanan ben Zakkai has bequeathed to it."

It seems strange that in Toynbee's view both the "way of Violence" and "the way of Gentleness" are actually one — namely the Zealotic way, as opposed to Herodianism. Granted that it was highly impractical, yes, suicidal, for Jewish rebels to oppose the superior power of the Roman armies, yet some will see heroism in the acts of fighters who preferred death to servitude. Be this as it may, no historian should close his ears to the still small voice of non-violence and self-renunciation acting in the name of something considered higher than a powerful state and "a triumphant alien force." It would seem that the mere fact of opposition to Hellenism is not sufficiently important to blur the difference between Violence and Mercy, between the militant and the peaceful. Hillel and Johanan ben Zakkai acted and thought as they did not merely as a reaction to Hellenism: They had an idea of right and wrong, of law and justice, independent of what "the formidable aggressor" thought. They lived humbly and did not shake fists at anyone; it is therefore misleading to present them among the Zealots, "shaking an infantile fist in an unimpressed Destiny's face."

Not only is it incorrect to speak of a Zealotism which supposedly includes men like Hillel and Johanan ben Zakkai; it is equally incorrect to speak of *one* Hellenism. Besides the Hellenism, represented by Herod and detested (and, to a large degree, ignored) by Hillel, there was a Hellenism which, as we have indicated, was consciously accepted, carefully integrated with Jewish thought and methods of thinking. The "historic collision between Hellenism and Jewry" was not resolved by the sword (fighting for or against Hellenism) but by the power of the spirit which works its way in history and, if need be, outside of it.

VIII

HILLEL'S PROSELYTES

It is commonly assumed that Judaism discourages proselytism, or at least is reluctant to accept converts. It is true that in the Middle Ages and up to modern times Judaism showed no interest in gaining proselytes. In Antiquity, however, the attitude was quite different. Hillel, especially, is remembered as a teacher sympathetic to those who wished to be guided into the Jewish faith.

The Whole Torah on One Foot

A certain heathen came to Shammai and said to him:
"If you can teach me the whole Torah while I stand on one foot, you can make me a Jew."
Shammai repulsed him with the builder's cubit which was in his hand.

He went to Hillel and Hillel said to him:
"What is hateful to you, do not do to your neighbor: that is the whole Torah; the rest is commentary; go, study."[1]

The first part of the answer ("What is hateful to you . . .") sounds like a short-cut to the core of religion, to a happy morality and to the good life. The addition, "Go, study" points to the long way that has to be taken, patiently and persistently. In order to recognize the other fellow as my neighbor, as my equal, as one who is like unto me, my naked, undirected Ego has to undergo radical change. Training of will-power, self-renunciation, loving understanding, is needed before a person will be ready to make room for the other. Such training is part of the study which cannot be done while one stands on one foot.

The goal is love; all men are brethren. A contemporary of Hillel puts it in these words:

> Ye see, my children, what great things I endured
> that I should not put my brethren to shame.
> Do ye also, love one another,
> and with long-suffering hide ye one another's faults.
> For God delighteth in the unity of brethren,
> and in the purpose of a heart that takes pleasure in
> love.[2]

Two More Proselytes

Another heathen wished to convert to Judaism if he were not required to accept the oral tradition in addition to the written Torah. Discouraged by Shammai, the man came to Hillel. Hillel patiently made him look upon oral communication as a natural part of the learning process and the heathen accepted the Torah as a whole.[3]

Still another heathen was attracted to Judaism by the pomp and ceremony accorded to the office of the high priest; it was his desire to reach this lofty goal. Again, Shammai was forthrightly discouraging; Hillel welcomed the man in the midst of Israel but had him study the rules of the office. Soon the proselyte realized that not even the king of Israel was eligible for the priesthood, the office being restricted to the descendants of Aaron. He was cured of his ambition; but in his studies he discovered other worthwhile aims and blessed Hillel for having led him on his way.

> Some time later the three proselytes met in one place.
> They said: "The irritability of Shammai wanted to drive us from the world:
> The forbearing of Hillel brought us under the wings of the divine presence."[4]

A later story tells that the grateful proselyte (the one who aspired to the high priesthood) begot two sons whom he called Hillel and Gamaliel; they were known as "Hillel's proselytes."[5]

Philo and the Talmudic Masters

These stories in which facts mingle with legend are told primarily not to emphasize the desirability of making proselytes or Hillel's portion in making proselytes and Shammai's objection to them, but to praise Hillel's forbearance as against Shammai's impatience. But the indirect evidence is an even clearer illustration of the attitude of classical Judaism to proselytism.

Philo of Alexandria considers converts "our friends and kinsmen, since they display that greatest of bonds to cement friendship, namely a pious and God-loving disposition." He notices that the lawgiver has given them equal rank and honor with born Jews.[6] Yet it is not only this Diaspora thinker who speaks in favor of converts. With a few exceptions,[7] talmudic masters sanction proselytism.

They say: "Beloved are converts, for Scripture applies to them the same terms as to Israel."[8] The word of the Prophet: "They that dwell under His shadow shall return" was understood to refer to the converts "who come and find protection in the shadow of the Lord" and the Lord says: "Their names are dear to me." A third-century teacher considered the proselyte dearer than the Israelites who saw the signs and wonders on Mount Sinai. "For the proselyte witnessed none of these signs and came and made his peace with (or: surrendered to) the Holy One, blessed be He, and took upon himself the Kingdom of Heaven; could a man be dearer than he?"

One of Hillel's converts aspired to the office of high priest and found the law against him. But the Sages taught that "the proselytes who study the Torah are considered equal to the high priest," for the Torah "does not speak of priest, Levite, Israelite, but of man"; therefore "one law and one ordinance shall be both for you and for the proselyte . . . ."[9]

Finally, pointing to the proselyte, the Midrash says:

There is no creature the Holy One, blessed be He, rejects,
but he accepts them all;
The gates are open at every hour,
and all who wish to enter, may enter.[10]

And, turning to the community of Israel, the Midrash has God saying:

Israel, you are a witness
"unto thee it was shown, that thou mightest know
   that the Lord is God,"
"Know this day . . . that there is none else";
Now, if you will not make known my divinity to
   the nations of the world,
you shall suffer for this iniquity.[11]

Most of the teachings just quoted come to us from
the first centuries of the Christian era. The attitude
to proselytism remained friendly and positive, even
though the missionary zeal had passed from Judaism
to the new religion. In Hillel's period proselytes were
not only welcome; the community was eager to make
converts. In the generation after Hillel, Helena, queen
of Adiabene (in Mesopotamia), and her sons Izates and
Monobaz embraced Judaism. The exclusiveness which
became more and more the fate of Judaism, still left
room to include all who wished to be included.

IX

A NOTE ON GREECE
AND ROME

We have noted a number of Greek, mainly Stoic,
parallels to Hillel's ethical teachings. More parallels
can be added. Hillel's saying, "If I am not for myself,
who is for me?" reminds one of Seneca's: "It is your
duty to try your best in everything if you wish to

succeed; there is no dependency upon others."[1] Timidity, which Hillel considers an obstacle to learning, appears also in Seneca's letters: "He who is too shy to ask for a teacher, shall never learn."[2]

Hillel's warning against a rash judgment of one's fellow reminds the reader of Seneca's word: "We should put ourselves in that place in which the man with whom we are angry is to be found."[3] Epictetus goes even a step further: "Give no judgment from another tribunal before you have yourself been judged at the tribunal of absolute justice."[4] Hillel cautions against saying: "When I shall have leisure I shall study," and Seneca gives this advice: "Do not excuse yourself with: I shall have leisure later and then I will seek wisdom."[5]

Hillel's serenity when hearing cries in his neighborhood echoes Horace, of Rome and Athens, contemporary of Hillel, who describes the wise man's serenity: "Even if the whole earth should break apart, the ruins would find the wise man without fear."[6]

Some may be led to conclude that there was a direct influence of Hellenist thought on Hillel and his disciples. Others may cautiously assume 'that here are parallel formulations of humanist thought common to all sensitive thinkers in late Antiquity. Both the Stoa and early classical Judaism maintain that it is not the politician, not the businessman, but the "wise man" who is the ideal type to be developed by education. *Paideia*, perfection through education, finds strong parallels in Judaism. The discipline of philosophy in Hellenism corresponds to the discipline of Torah in

Judaism. The one sees the source of moral action in human reason, the other in the divine will; common to both is the moral action, the accent on the ethical imperative and on self-perfection.

The most significant term in Greek thought is *logos*, word, saying, speech, the rational principle in the universe and the utterance of God. In human use *logos* is, in the words of Gilbert Murray, "the great substitute for violence"; it is the instrument of discourse, argument and persuasion. The parallels in Judaism are obvious, both on the level of religious thought and of personal ethics and social legislation. The basic method of the Talmud is rational argument and dialectic analysis of the text.

Yet, classical Judaism excluded itself from the universalism prevailing at the time in the ancient world. To understand this act of exclusion, so crucial for later Jewish history, some of the differences between classical Judaism and the schools of late Hellenism should be considered.

The philosophies of late Antiquity were directed to the intelligentsia and the leisure class of the cities; classical Judaism felt the responsibility for a whole people. The wise man, the scholar, the Hasid, were ideal types, but they existed for the people. Hillel counteracted the sectarian tendencies in Judaism, opposed the individual's separation from the community at large. The Hasid was not at liberty to escape into the desert or into the solitude of his chamber.

The Stoics and the Epicureans, each with different emphasis, taught *apatheia*, the attitude of indifference towards, and independence of, whatever may disturb the quietude of the wise man's inner life, and *ataraxia*, looking at all things with an equanimity of mind. Although Epictetus taught that only he who is aware of his misery and his weakness could understand the philosopher, the schools did not leave room for commiseration with the indigent or pity for the poor. Classical Judaism, on the other hand, was not satisfied with social legislation and philanthropic organization but taught the charity of the heart, offering one's own soul to the poor; the attitude of compassion and deeds of loving-kindness was not only an expression of humaneness; it was *imitatio dei*.

Posidonius, the most influential of the thinkers in the Middle Stoa, professed the continual communion between the world of God and the world of man, and spoke of moral and political activity as of a religious duty. Nevertheless, the Stoa and the other systems of thought in late Antiquity were philosophies, not religions. Unlike classical Judaism, they could not know of the "broken and contrite heart," of the sinner who prays for forgiveness and for strength to return nor of the merciful God, ready to receive those who turn to him.

The theoretically impressive moral teachings of detachment by the philosophical schools are strangely combined with instructions for advantageous money-making and with assiduous profiteering by some of their representatives. Seneca's advocacy of independence of circumstances, pain and death clashes with his repeatedly exhibited cowardice and dishonesty. The modern explanation of this inconsistency, that Seneca was a neurotic personality, would have sounded hollow in the ears of a contemporary Jew. In Judaism, only practice makes the theory possible; many words lead to sin.

These differences may explain, at least partly, what prompted classical Judaism to remain a separate entity in the ancient world.

A closer historical analysis might suggest that the relationship between Judea and Hellas would have been much closer, and of greater cultural consequences, had not Rome assumed the tutelage of Greece. Greece had much that appealed to the intelligent Jew. And, indeed, both Judea and the Jewish diaspora had, since Alexander, accepted some quite important Greek concepts and methods and adapted them to their own culture. This process, the beginning of which we observed in the third century B. C. E., did not come to an end even in Hillel's time. Now, however, the "outside world" was no longer represented by the Greeks and their philosophers, but by Rome and its governors; even Greek philosophy now appeared in a Roman version.

The subjected peoples, more than the Romans themselves, were fascinated by the authority of the Empire and believed in the *Roma aeterna*, a concept which persisted into the sixteenth century. Yet, about the middle of the first pre-Christian century, Cicero started to lament the death of freedom in Rome. This Rome, to be sure, appealed to some careerists and seekers after material advantage. For a thinking Jerusalemite

Rome could not have any attraction. Posidonius'
glorification of the Roman commonwealth of mankind,
as a reflection of the commonwealth of God, did not
ring true in the ears of Hillel's contemporaries. Mem-
ories of some Seleucid rulers, of some Hasmoneans,
and experiences with Herod and his successors con-
vinced them that politics was corrupt and could not be
equated with morality as the Roman had done. The
world of politics appeared less and less divinely
intended. More and more, the divine was sought and
found in the human soul and in the just community
of men.

X

HILLEL'S DEATH AND THE RISE OF JOHANAN BEN ZAKKAI

Hillel's Death

Hillel had spoken of the poor soul which is but a
guest in the body, here on earth today only, and gone
tomorrow;[1] he knew of the transitoriness of life. He
had said: "Trust not yourself until the day of your
death";[2] he knew of the vicissitudes of spiritual
growth. Now, the end was approaching, and the
disciples assembled around the master for a final word
or a blessing. They were led by Jonathan ben Uzziel,
the translator of prophetic books, he "who had revealed
the Lord's secrets to man.".

Such a scene, recorded first in the story of Hillel, repeats itself later in classical Judaism, so in the tale of Johanan ben Zakkai ("O master, bless us!"), in the drama of Hanina ben Teradion ("O master, what do you see?"), and in the tale of Akiba's martyrdom ("O master, can you still carry in love the yoke of the Kingdom of Heaven?").

All disciples had entered Hillel's chambers but one, Johanan ben Zakkai, who had humbly remained in the courtyard. Hillel asked: "Where is he, the youngest among you, he who is destined to be the father of wisdom and the father of the generations to come?" They brought him in. When Hillel saw him, he quoted the words of personified Wisdom in the *Book of Proverbs*: "I will endow with substance those who love me and fill their treasuries."[3]

When Hillel died, they recalled the strange meeting in Jericho (which we have tentatively placed at the beginning of the road). There a mysterious voice spoke of the sage as worthy of the holy spirit if only his generation would deserve him. Maybe the generation was worthy of him, after all. The disciples remembered the master's life and alluded to the three themes to which he had dedicated it. They said:

"The Hasid, the humble man, the disciple of Ezra [is no more]."[4]

Johanan ben Zakkai, the Disciple

Hillel's work made possible a reconstruction of Judaism after the fall of Jerusalem in 70 C. E. His youngest disciple, Johanan ben Zakkai, assumed the leadership of the remnant.

Before Jerusalem fell, Johanan left the besieged city, appeared before the Roman general, Vespasian, acknowledged his sovereignty and asked his permission to maintain a school in Jabneh (near Jaffa and Lydda). Johanan's non-political stand before Vespasian, reminiscent of Hillel's attitude toward Herod, enabled him to rescue a center of learning that was to carry on the heritage and the hopes of Jerusalem.

To his disciples grieving over the loss of the atoning worship in the Jerusalem temple, Johanan ben Zakkai gave an answer which employed the Hillelite *hesed* motif: "Do not grieve; we have another atonement as great as this: it is acts of mercy, for the prophet Hosea said, I desire loving-kindness (*hesed*) and not sacrifice."[5]

To Johanan ben Zakkai, as to Hillel, *hesed* meant the advance of the right relationship between man and man, in the family, in the school, in the city and among nations; on this and no other basis can the community of man be established. The law of the Jewish community in Judea was the Torah in its widest sense, and in interpreting it, Johanan used the method of *midrash*, like his master. And like Hillel, Johanan ben Zakkai lived with and for his disciples, whom he wanted to be fountains, not reservoirs. He asked them "go forth and see which is the good way for man"; from among their answers he chose the simplest: "A good heart."[6] He believed that the divine word on Sinai desired to make man free and that he who hears this word never "should go and sell himself into slavery" and recognize another person as his master.[7] Here Johanan ben Zakkai follows Hillel's emphasis on human dignity.

Such quiet, undemonstrative, faithful work grew out of Hillel's school; it was strong enough to hold its ground against the violent outbursts of men like the anonymous author of *The Fourth Book of Ezra* who saw in Jerusalem's catastrophe a sign of universal disaster. The escape into apocalyptic visions in Johanan ben Zakkai's time corresponded to the retreat into the wilderness in former generations and the flight into Zealotic nationalism in the war against Rome. Classical Judaism did not react negatively to catastrophe; it put no trust in the sword, and, in national defeat, knew of no visions of hopelessness. These acts, classical Judaism counteracted by its Halakhah which taught discipline of life, individual and communal, and by cultivating loyalty to enduring values, defined as mercy, learning, and simple faith.

EPILOGUE: CLASSICAL
JUDAISM

In sketching the emergence of classical Judaism —
I avoid the term "normative Judaism" as historically
misleading — we have reversed the order followed by
Hillel in his dialogue with the heathen. We have first
studied the sources (or, at least, a good part of them)
and may now be permitted to summarize the main
points.

Classical Judaism, as it emerges in Hillel, stands
first of all for Torah: its source is the divine revelation
to Israel, but its application to the ever-changing conditions of life is in the hands of man; rational knowledge
is the tool by which man may approach the law. Under
the law, all aspects of life are important; there is no
artificial separation between a "sacred" and a "secular"
realm of life.

Classical Judaism emphasizes learning, which is more
than an instrument for the increase of factual knowledge. The Torah is more than a book; the teacher
more than a dispenser, the disciple more than a
recipient of information. The study of the Torah is a
living bridge between the divine and the human.

In dealing with a fellow-man and with society,
classical Judaism requires more than justice: it requires
hesed, acts of loyalty, mercy, loving concern, a spirit of
renunciation and conciliation. The poor should be

helped and the underprivileged protected: by laws and statutes, and by the loving attitude of their fellow-man. By actions of *hesed*, man emulates God.

The law imposes a wide range of obligations; wide is the field of learning. Yet, all can be reduced to one simple principle, be it Hillel's "What is hateful to you, do not do to your neighbor," or Akiba's restatement of Leviticus, "Love thy neighbor as thyself," or Ben Azzai's "In the likeness of God He made Man," or Bar Kappara's "In all thy ways know Him," or Simlai's, "The righteous lives by his faith." Only if such a basic core, underlying all variations, is clearly seen, the minutiae of the law will not lead to confusion.

Classical Judaism developed in opposition to power-politics, militarism, and the deterioration of the official priesthood. It remained critical of these forces; it did not entrust itself to the forces of history; it chose to remain powerless. It hopes patiently for the Messianic redemption as the last stage before the universal Kingdom of God. This kingdom can be anticipated in the community of Israel and in the synagogue, its liturgy, its Sabbaths and festivals.

Man, in classical Judaism, loves God, creator of heaven and earth, father of mankind; he knows that God's love penetrates the whole world and reaches into man's heart. He moves in an atmosphere of divine love. God, concerned with man, rewards and punishes, but never rejects man; there is *teshuvah*, the possibility of return.

Classical Judaism welcomed proselytes and accorded

them equality of rights. But it was not equipped to go out and convert the world.

I hasten to add that this is a rough and by necessity incomplete list of main factors and not a catechism. What is important is the harmonious combination of these factors and the comparative simplicity of their function. Hillel lacks the profundity of the author of the *Book of Job* before him, and the virtuosity and acumen of the talmudic masters after him; but he is closer to the common man and to a living community and its needs.

We have seen parallels between Hillel and the sectarian Dead Sea movements in the emphasis on learning (in a specific sense), on Scriptural exegesis (*midrash*), on the Sabbath, on mercy and loving-kindness, on the rights of the poor, on inwardness, on simplicity and quietude. We have further seen some cardinal points where Hillel appears in opposition to the sects: he rejected their radical view of the just *versus* the wicked, good *versus* evil and advocated a middle line; against their strict rulings, he advocated leniency; his religious outlook removed him from the ardent and urgent Messianism of the sects; and, most decisive, Hillel rejected the very basis of sectarianism, the withdrawal into the desert and the sects' pronounced individualism; instead, Hillel tried to revive the true and just community (as against the state) for which he found a model and a paradigm in Early Hasidism. This re-orientation in Judaism was Hillel's achievement.

And it is significant that, despite its tendency to

extremism and occasional overemphasis on one aspect
or another, Judaism itself (and not merely its later
historians) should have recognized Hillel as the man who
"reestablished the forgotten Torah." Thus Hillel's
teachings, though in various degrees rooted in ages
past, could appear as representative of emerging classical Judaism, a period which — roughly speaking —
came to an end in the third century. By that time
Judaism was well prepared for its long journey.

NOTES

For the scholarly reader

I

THE HISTORICAL AND CULTURAL BACKGROUND

[1] On Herod: Josephus, *Antiquities*, XIV–XVII; *Wars*, I, 10–33.

[2] On the Early Hasidim: I. F. Baer, "The Historical Foundations of the Halacha," *Zion*, XVII (1952); "The Ancient Hasidim in Philo's Writings and in Hebrew Tradition," *Zion*, XVIII (1953); *Israel Among the Nations*, Jerusalem 1955 (all in Hebrew).

[3] *Quod Omnis Probus Liber Sit*, XII and XIII.

[4] Josephus, *Wars*, II. 8.

[5] *Ibid.*, II. 8. 7.

[6] *Probus*, XII. The F. H. Colson translation (The Loeb Classical Library) has been consulted.

[7] II. 24–25; V. 3–4. These and the following passages (X 18, 26; XI. 1) are quoted in the translation of William H. Brownlee, *The Dead Sea Manual of Discipline*, American Schools of Oriental Research, 1951.

II

HILLEL'S BEGINNINGS AND HIS ASCENT

[1] Yer. Pesahim 33a.

[2] Yoma 35b. For the renditions from the Babylonian Talmud the Soncino translation (ed. by I. Epstein, London 1935 seq.) has been consulted.

[3] See Sotah 21a.

[4] Yer. Pesahim 33a.

[5] L. Finkelstein, *The Pharisees and the Men of the Great Synagogue* (Hebrew), 1950, ch. I.

[6] Mishnah Hagigah II. 2.

[7] Yer. Hagigah 77d; L. Ginzberg, *On Jewish Law and Lore*, 1955, p. 101.

[8] See Finkelstein, *op. cit.*, p. 83.

[9] As masters of *tradition* Hillel and Shammai succeeded Shemaiah and Abtalion and brought the so-called period of the "pairs" to a conclusion before the start of the era of the Tannaites. See Ginzberg, *op. cit.*, p. 102.

[10] Sifre on Deuteronomy 34.7.

[11] Berakhot 63a.

[12] Soferim XVI. 9.

[13] Sukkah 20a.

[14] Tosefta Sotah XIII. 3; Sotah 48b. Such a scene is reported again in connection with a disciple of Hillel in Jabneh, the center of learning after the fall of Jerusalem.

[15] This and the following quotations: Abot II. 4, I. 14, I. 12.

III

THE WAYS AND BELIEFS OF THE HASID

[1] See Adolf Büchler, *Types of Jewish Palestinian Piety from 70 B. C. E. to 70 C. E.*, 1922.

[2] Berakhot 60a, quoting Psalm 112.7.

[3] Betzah 16a, quoting Psalm 68.20.

[4] Abot II. 6.

[5] *Testament of Zebulun* 54.4.

[6] Epictetus, *Discourses* IV. 11.2.

[7] This and the next story: Leviticus Rabbah XXXIV. 3.

[8] Josephus, *Wars*, II. 8.11.

[9] Baba Metzia 49a.

[10] Berakhot 28a.

[11] Ketubot 16bf.

[12] Tosefta Berakhot II. 21; cf. Derekh Eretz Zutta V.

[13] Shabbat 30 bf.

[14] On the "ceremony of Water-Drawing": Mishnah Sukkah V. 4; Sukkah 53a; Yer. Sukkah 55b; Abot de Rabbi Nathan II, ch. XXVII.

IV

THE COMMON MAN AND THE POOR

[1] *Enoch* 94.8, 10; 95.7; 96.1; 97.1; 98.3, 10, 13; 99.10–16; 102.4; 103.3; 104.2.

[2] Tosefta Sanhedrin XIII. 3; Rosh ha-Shanah 16b. Quotations: Zechariah 13.9, I Samuel 2.6.

[3] *Quod Omnis Probus Liber Sit*, XII.

[4] Josephus, *Wars*, II. 8.3.

[5] *Manual of Discipline*, IX. 21–23.

[6] *Habakkuk Commentary*, XII. 3–6; Commentary on Psalm 37.22.

[7] *Psalms of Solomon* 10.7.

[8] *Derekh Eretz* VI.

[9] Taanit 23b.

[10] Ketubot 67b.

[11] Sifre on Deuteronomy 15.9.

[12] Leviticus Rabbah I. 5.

[13] Midrash Tehillim on 86.1.

[14] Shabbat 88b.

V

LEARNING

[1] *Hypothetica* 7.13. See also *Quod Deus Sit Immutabilis* 24; on the contemplative life of study, see *De Specialibus Legibus* IV. 26; II. 15; *De Fuge et Inventione* 6. Cicero, on the other hand, prefers the *vita civilis* of the statesman to the *vita quieta* of the sage. *De Re Publica* II. 3.

[2] *Manual of Discipline*, VI. 6–8.

[3] *Ibid.*, VIII. 12–16.

[4] *Zadokite Documents*, VII. 18.

[5] *Manual of Discipline*, IX. 16–21.

[6] *Ibid.*, VIII. 13; IX. 20–21.

[7] Abot I. 1, 4, 11.

[8] This and the following quotations: Abot II. 5; II 4; II 7; I. 13.

[9] Abot de Rabbi Nathan II, ch. I, beginning.

[10] *Ibid.*, ch. XXVI.

[11] Hagigah 9b, quoting Malachi 3.18.

[12] This and the following quotations: Plutarch, *De Exilio* 5; *De Stoicorum Repugnantiis* I; Epictetus, *Dissertationes* IV. 3.9–12.

[13] Sources for this section: Pesahim 54a; Sifre on Deuteronomy 11:10; Genesis Rabbah I.2; I.6; Abodah Zarah 3b; Mekhilta on Exodus 19.2; Shabbat 88b; Sifre on Deuteronomy 33.2; Abot VI.2; Mekhilta on Exodus 13.3; Deuteronomy Rabbah IV.4; Genesis Rabbah LXVI.2.

[14] *Legum Allegoria* 1, 93f. See H. A. Wolfson, *Philo*, 1947, II, ch. XII.

[15] Deuteronomy 24.6; the following interpretation, Mishnah Baba Metzia IX.13.

[16] Hillel is the first teacher to whom the use of the term "oral law" is found ascribed. See E. H. Weiss, *Dor Dor ve-Doreshav*, III, 24b.

VI

THE TWO RIVAL SCHOOLS

[1] L. Ginzberg, *On Jewish Law and Lore*, 1955; L. Finkelstein, *The Pharisees*, 1946. Our records list over 300 controversies between the two schools; in about 50 cases the Shammaiites followed a more moderate view than the Hillelites.

[2] Abot de Rabbi Nathan I, ch. III.

[3] Mishnah Berakhot VIII.1; see Ginzberg, *op. cit.*, pp. 105f.

[4] Mishnah Rosh ha-Shanah I.1; see Ginzberg, *op. cit.*, pp. 117f.

[5] Sources for this section: Mishnah Kiddushin II.1; Mishnah Yebamot XIII.1; Deuteronomy 24.1; Mishnah Gittin IX.10; Mishnah Eduyot IV.7.

[6] See Mishnah Eduyot V.3; Shabbat 30b. A similar controversy took place about the *Book of Proverbs*.

[7] See Shabbat 13b. L. Ginzberg, *The Legends*, VI, p. 422.

[8] Sources for this section: Hagigah 12a; cf. Genesis Rabbah I.15 and XII.12, 14; Erubin 13b.

[9] Yebamot 14b, quoting Zechariah 8.19.

[10] This and the next quotations: Erubin 13b; Abot V.17; Mishnah Eduyot I.4; Sanhedrin 88b.

VII

COMMUNITY VS. STATE

[1] Leo Baeck, *The Pharisees and Other Essays*, 1947, p. 47. The transition from the rule of kings to the guidance by teachers is indicated in a midrash reinterpreting Genesis 49.10; Sanhedrin 5a.

[2] Abot I.12.

[3] Mekhilta on Exodus 20.25.

[4] Josephus, *Antiquities*, XIV.2.1.

[5] Sources for this section: Deuteronomy 15.1–11; Mishnah Shebiit X.3; Gittin 34b; Leviticus 25; Mishnah Arakhin IX.5.

[6] Shabbat 21b.

[7] See Baba Batra 134a.

[8] See Megillah 3a.

[9] This and the following quotations: *A Study of History*, vol. VIII, pp. 580–583; vol. V, pp. 74–75.

VIII

HILLEL'S PROSELYTES

[1] Shabbat 31a. Jesus quotes the Golden Rule in a positive formulation (Matthew 7.12); yet early Christian writings outside the Gospels prefer the negative version because of its strong practical appeal. Isocrates in the West and Confucius in the East use the negative formulation.

[2] *The Testament of Joseph* 17:1–3.

[3] Shabbat 31a.

[4] *Ibid.*, quoting Exodus 28.4, Numbers 1.51, Exodus 4.22.

[5] Abot de Rabbi Nathan I, ch. XV.

[6] *De Poenitentia* I; *De Monarchia* I.7.

[7] E. g., "Proselytes are as hard on Israel as leprosy," Yebamot 47b.

[8] This and the following quotations: Mekhilta on Exodus 22.20; Leviticus Rabbah I.2, quoting Hosea 14.8; Midrash Tanhuma on Genesis 14.1.

[9] Leviticus 18.5; Numbers 15.16; Tanhuma Yelamdenu on Exodus 37.1.

[10] Exodus Rabbah XIX.4.

[11] Leviticus Rabbah VI.5.

IX

A NOTE ON GREECE AND ROME

[1] Seneca, *Epistulae morales* XXVII.

[2] Seneca, *Letter* L.

[3] Seneca, *De Ira* III, 12.

[4] Epictetus, *Fragments* LV.

[5] Seneca, *Letters* XVII and LXXII.

[6] For these and other parallels, see A. Kaminka, "Hillel's Life and Work," *The Jewish Quarterly Review*, N. S., XXX, pp. 107–122.

X

HILLEL'S DEATH AND THE RISE OF JOHANAN BEN ZAKKAI

[1] Leviticus Rabbah XXXIV.3.

[2] Abot II.4.

[3] Proverbs 8.21.

[4] Yer. Nedarim 39b; Sanhedrin 11a.

[5] Abot de Rabbi Nathan I, ch. IV, quoting Hosea 6.6.

[6] Abot II.9.

[7] Kiddushin 22b.

CHRONOLOGICAL SUMMARY

B. C. E.

538–516	Return from the Babylonian Exile and rebuilding of the Temple. Beginning of Second Commonwealth.
444	Ezra the Scribe announces the Torah as the constitution of Judea (traditional date).
332	After Alexander the Great: Start of Hellenistic domination. Rise of Stoicism and Epicureanism.
4th-3rd cent.	Early Hasidim.
c. 260	Translation of the Pentateuch into Greek (the *Septuagint*).
198–167	Judea under the rule of the Syrian Seleucids.
190	Battle of Magnesia: Roman power extends to the Orient.
166–164	Maccabean rebellion. *The Book of Daniel.*
146	Rome ends Greek independence.
142	Judea regains independence under the rule of Simon the Hasmonean.
142–63	The rule of the Hasmoneans.
2nd cent.	Rise of Sadducees and Pharisees. *The Wisdom of Solomon.*
103–76	Reign of Alexander Jannaeus.
76–67	Reign of Salome Alexandra.
67	Civil war between Aristobulus II and Hyrcanus II.
1st cent.	The Essenes; Dead Sea Sect. The *Zadokite Documents* and the *Manual of Discipline.*
1st cent.	*The Book of Enoch, The Psalms of Solomon, The Book of Jubilees, Testaments of the Twelve Patriarchs.*
63	Pompey enters Jerusalem. Judea tributary to Romans. (31 B. C. E., Battle of Actium; final triumph of the Roman Empire; Egypt becomes Roman province).
c. 60	Birth of Hillel.
c. 40	Hillel comes to Jerusalem.

37–4	Reign of Herod the Great.
31	Earthquake in Judea.
c. 30	Hillel comes again to Jerusalem.
c. 4	Birth of Jesus.
4 B.C.E.–34 C.E.	Reign of Herod's sons.
c. 30 B.C.E. — 40 C.E.	Philo of Alexandria.
C. E.	
c. 10	Death of Hillel.
38–c.100	Flavius Josephus.
66–73	The war against the Romans. Destruction of Jerusalem. *The Fourth Book of Ezra.*
c. 67	Death of Paul, apostle to the Gentiles.
c. 70	Johanan ben Zakkai. The new school of Jabneh.
115–117	Insurrection against Rome.
132–135	Revolt of Bar Kokhba. Rabbi Akiba.
c. 200	Final redaction of the *Mishnah*.

SUGGESTIONS
FOR FURTHER STUDY

The vast historic background for Hillel's era and activities is treated in Elias J. Bickerman, "The Historical Foundations of Postbiblical Judaism," *The Jews*, ed. Louis Finkelstein, Vol. I (Philadelphia 1949); Robert H. Pfeiffer, *History of New Testament Times* (New York 1949); Salo W. Baron, *A Social and Religious History of the Jews*, second edition, Vol. I and II (New York 1952). In Hebrew: Joseph Klausner, *Toledot ha-Bayit ha-Sheni*, Vol. IV (Jerusalem 1952).

On Hillel: Judah Goldin, "Hillel the Elder," *The Journal of Religion* (1946); Armand Kaminka, "Hillel's Life and Work," *The Jewish Quarterly Review*, New Series, Vol. XXX (1939–1940).

On Pharisaism, Talmud, classical Judaism: Leo Baeck, *The Pharisees* (New York 1947); Louis Finkelstein, *The Pharisees* (2 vols., Philadelphia 1938); Louis Ginzberg, "The Significance of the Halachah for Jewish History," *On Jewish Law and Lore* (Philadelphia 1955); Judah Goldin, "The Period of the Talmud," *The Jews*, ed. Louis Finkelstein, Vol. I; R. Travers Herford, *The Pharisees* (London 1924); George Foot Moore, *Judaism in the First Centuries of the Christian Era* (3 vols., Cambridge, Mass. 1927–1930); Max Weber, *Ancient Judaism*, Part V: The Pharisees (Glencoe, Ill. 1952); Solomon Zeitlin, *The Sadducees and the Pharisees* (Philadelphia 1937); Louis Ginzberg, *Legends of the Jews* (7 vols., index volume by Boaz Cohen, Philadelphia 1909–1938); M. Mielziner, *Introduction to the Talmud* (Third Edition, New York 1925); Hermann Strack, *Introduction to the Talmud* (Philadelphia 1931).

Hellenistic Judaism may be studied in: Erwin R. Goodenough, *By Light, Light: the Mystic Gospel of Hellenistic Judaism* (New Haven 1935). A penetrating evaluation of Philo is Harry Austryn Wolfson's, *Philo* (2 vols., Cambridge, Mass. 1947). The standard edition of the text of Philo's works with an English translation is by F. H. Colson, G. H. Whitaker, and Ralph Marcus, in Loeb Classical Library (ii vols., London,

New York and Cambridge, Mass. 1929 seq.). On Flavius Josephus see Norman Bentwich, *Josephus* (Philadelphia 1926); Henry St. J. Thackeray, *Josephus, the Man and the Historian* (New York 1929). The standard edition of the text of Josephus' works with an English translation is by Henry St. J. Thackeray and Ralph Marcus, in Loeb Classical Library (1926 seq.).

Comprehensive surveys of the apocryphal writings are: Charles Torrey, *The Apocryphal Literature* (New Haven 1945); Solomon Zeitlin, "The Apocrypha," *The Jewish Quarterly Review* XXXVII (1947); also, the second part of Robert H. Pfeiffer, *History of New Testament Times* (New York 1949). An English translation with notes is edited by R. H. Charles, *The Apocrypha and Pseudepigrapha of the Old Testament* (2 vols., Oxford 1913).

For information on the Dead Sea sects see Millar Burrows, *The Dead Sea Scrolls* (New York 1955) and *More Light on the Dead Sea Scrolls* (New York 1958); A. Dupont-Sommer, *The Jewish Sect of Qumran and the Essenes* (New York 1955); T. H. Gaster, *The Dead Sea Scriptures* (New York 1956); C. Rabin, *Qumran Studies* (London 1957); F. M. Cross, Jr., *The Ancient Library of Qumran* (New York 1958).